OCT 2020

Recycling

by Anne Giulieri

raintree
a Capstone company — publishers for children

Have a good look around your house.

Can you see paper that you do not need?

Can you see some **glass** jars too?

Look at the old **plastic** bottles.

3

Will you throw them away?

Have a look outside.

Can you see some old car **tyres**?

If you look around, you will always find lots of things that you don't need. Old paper, glass jars, plastic bottles and tyres can all be made into something new!

6

This is called
recycling.

7

Here is some old paper.
The paper can be sent
to a big **factory** and
made into new paper.

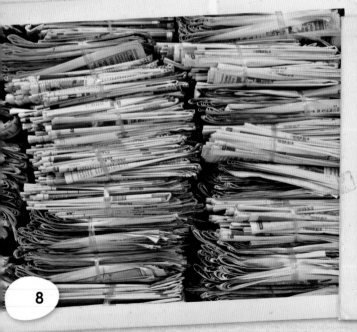

This little girl is recycling some old paper.

She is writing on it and making it into a book.

Here are some glass jars.
They can be recycled.
They can be made into
new glass at a factory.

You can put flowers and pens into old glass jars.

Here are some old plastic bottles.
They can be recycled. The plastic
bottles are taken to a factory.
They can be made into **fences**,
plastic bags and bottles.

You can reuse old plastic bottles.
They can be made into pots
for plants.

Here are some old tyres. The old tyres can be recycled. This swing is made from an old tyre.

Look at the playground.
The ground has been
made from old tyres too.

Old tyres

Look around your house.
Can you recycle too?

Glossary

fence barrier that divides areas of land
factory place where things are made or built
glass a hard, see-through material used to make things such as windows, jars and glasses

plastic material that can be easily shaped when soft
tyre rubber wheel found on a car or lorry

Index